Celestia 1.6
Beginners Guide

Thomas Ecclestone

ISBN-13: 978-1500758691
ISBN-10: 1500758698

DEDICATION

This book is dedicated to Gabriel Bogo, without whom it wouldn't have been written!

CONTENTS

1 INSTALLING CELESTIA

1 Google "Install Celestia" using your favorite browser

2 Click on Celestia – Sourceforge

3 Click on Download

4 You may have to wait for a few seconds for the download to star

5 Once the download has started you will see the following box:

6 Wait until the download has finished.

7 Click on

8 Click on "Open"

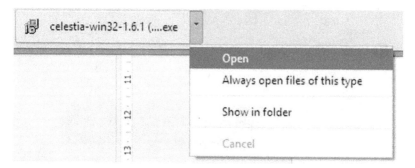

9 Select "Yes" in the windows dialogue asking if you want to make

changes to the computer

10 The Installation dialogue will open. Click Next

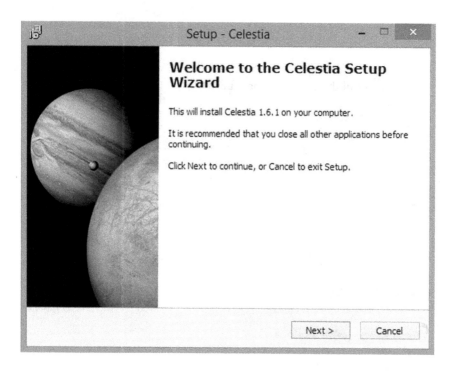

⓫ Check ◉ I accept the agreement then ⟨ Next > ⟩

⓬ If you want to change the installation directory

①Press Browse

To continue, click Next. If you would like to select a different folder, click Browse.

C:\Program Files (x86)\Celestia   Browse...

②Select a folder from the list

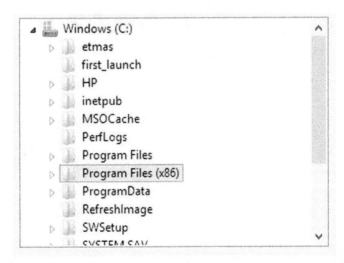

③Select

⓭ When you have the correct installation directory selected, press

⓮ the next screen gives you the option of changing the Start Menu

folder. I recommend just pressing Next >

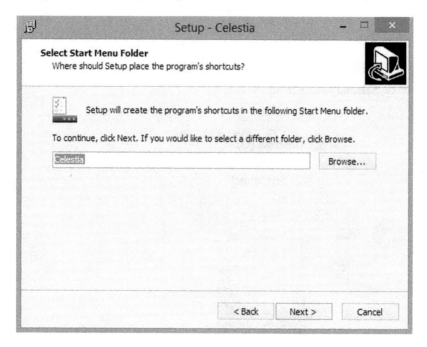

⓯The next dialogue asks if you want to associate file types with

Celestia. I recommend selecting Next >

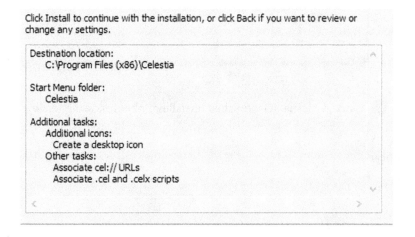

16 Finally, the setup program will display all the options you have

selected.

① If you are happy with them select Install

② If you are not happy with them select either < Back to change

your selections or if you decide not to install Celestia after all.

⓱ A progress dialogue will appear

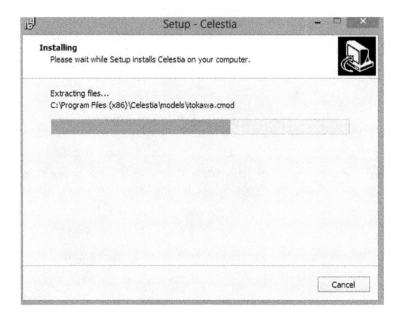

⓲ Once Celestia has finished installing, the following dialogue will

appear

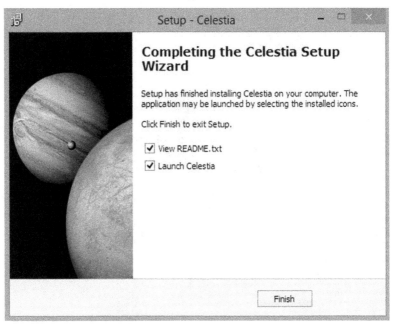

① uncheck ☑ View README.txt if you do not want to display information

about celestia when you finish installation

② uncheck ☑ Launch Celestia if you do not want to start Celestia directly

after installation

③ Press [Finish] to finish the installation.

④ If you opted to launch Celestia after installation it should start up.

(5) To start it from the desktop doubleclick on the Celestia icon

2 STARTING TO USE CELESTIA

MENU BAR

File Navigation Time Render View Bookmarks Help

The menu bar is at the top of the screen. It provides you with most of the commands that you need in order to use Celestia.

I've written a short description of each menu below, but we will go into each option in more depth latter in the book.

FILE MENU

The File menu gives you the ability to run scripts, capture images or movies and exit the program.

Open Script Opens a script
Scripts Select a script to run
Capture Image takes a screenshot of viewable area
Capture Movie Records a movie of viewable area

Scripts are an interesting feature in Celestia. They allow you to write short programs that can affect how Celestia displays the universe, and do anything that you would otherwise do manually.

NAVIGATION MENU

You will spend the most time on the Navigation Menu. It is here that you select objects, goto objects, and move your point of view around the known universe. Select Sol is a special option on this menu as it allows you to select the sun.

There are three main types of option within the navigation menu

Selection – chose an object to goto, center the viewpoint around, or track

Go to – Go to a selected object

Automatic movement – Follow, Track, or Sync Orbits with your selected object.

In addition there are Freeflight movements available with the mouse or keyboard shortcuts which allow you to control navigation without referencing a selected object.

The next chapter will focus on some basic navigation.

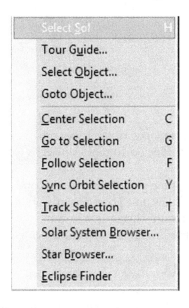

Select Sol Select the sun
Tour Guide A tour of notable locations
Select Object Select object by name
Goto Object Goto any object

Centre Selection middle of viewable area
Goto Selection Goto current selection
Follow Selection lock onto object
Sync Orbit Selection remain above selection
Track Selection stays on object
Solar system Browser items in solar system
Star Browser Nearby stars
Eclipse Finder List eclipses

TIME MENU

Celestia allows you to view the universe not just as it is in the present moment but also at almost any time in the present or past. You can speed up the rate that time is flowing on the display, set it, slow it down or even reverse it.

The time menu provides many of these commands.

10x Faster Make time got 10 times faster
10 x Slower Make time go 10 times slower
Freeze Freeze time
Real Time Make time go at 1 second a second
Reverse Time Makes time go backwards
Set Time Sets time to whenever you want
Show Local Time display the local time

RENDER MENU

The Render menu is used to control the amount of detail that Celestia shows, including grid lines, how many stars are visible, features on planets and moons, how rough or smooth the graphics will display and what resolution the textures will be displayed as.

In some cases the options may require more work from the processor.

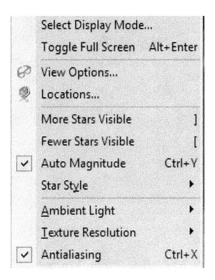

Mode... Select resolution
Toggle Make viewable area full screen
View Options Control stellar options
Locations Control planetary options
More Stars Visible display more stars
Fewer Stars Visible display less stars
Auto Magnitude controls star visibility
Star Style controls how stars are displayed
Ambient Light how much light is in shadows
Texture Resolution controls detail of textures
Antialiasing Smooth out some graphics

VIEW MENU

The View menu allows you to control how many frames are displayed at once. You can divide the screen horizontally or vertically looking at the same object from different locations or even making time flow differently in different views.

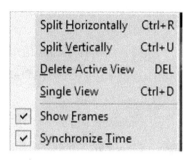

Horizontally Divide into two horizontal frames
Vertically Divide into Vertical frame
Delete remove current frame
Single remove all except current frame
Show Frames toggle frames on or off
Synchronize both frames set to same time

BOOKMARKS MENU

The Bookmarks menu allows you to store your current viewpoint so you can easily return to it without having to remember long chains of commands. You can also modify existing bookmarks.

Add Create a bookmark at current location
Organize Modify, delete or move bookmarks

HELP MENU

The Help menu allows you to run a demo displaying many of the features of Celestia, run the online help, and gives you information about license terms and Celestia.

Run Displays a demo showing Celestia's features
User Guide provides online help
Controls Informs you of Celestia's controls
OpenGL Licensing info for OpenGL
License Your license information
About all about Celestia

VIEWABLE AREA

The viewable Area displays information about the universe at the time and in the location of your current viewpoint. Notice that in all four corners there can be information about your current viewpoint location.

- Selection Information
- Time
- Speed
- Automatic Movement

When you open Celestia you are moved to a fixed location away from the earth, at the current time, are not moving and are following earth.

Your commands will change all this information.

SELECTION INFORMATION

In the top left hand of the screen Celestia displays information about your current selection. In this case you are just over 31km from earth.

Earth
Distance: 31,891 km
Radius: 6,378.1 km
Apparent diameter: 19° 11' 17.3"
Phase angle: 7.2°

TIME INFORMATION

On the top left hand of the screen Celestia displays the time it is rendering right now, and whether time has been frozen, is in real time (one second a second) or is faster or slower than real time. A minus sign means that time is going backwards.

2014 May 22 11:56:21 UTC
Real time

SPEED INFORMATION

Speed information shows how fast you are moving right now. Celestia displays it at the bottom left hand of the screen. You can increase or decrease your speed – I'll describe how in the Navigation chapter.

NAVIGATION INFORMATION

 Celestia give you the option to move automatically, so that you remain in the same position over your selection. Automatic movement is recorded on the bottom right hand of the screen.

NEXT CHAPTER

This chapter has tried to explain what's going on in the first screen you see but naturally you'll be eager to start using the program. The next chapter gets to the meat – how to use Celestia to view anywhere on earth, and also go to the Moon!

3 TRIP TO THE MOON

This chapter provides a short tutorial for the program. It focuses on the most basic features of the program allowing you to get started right away. By the end of this chapter you should know:

How to go to any latitude, longitude and distance over the earth

How to go to any Planet in the Solar System and

How to go to any Moon or Satellite that Celestia has information about.

It's a short chapter, but I hope that you enjoy your short tour of the Moon!

❶ Running Celestia

If you are not yet running Celestia double click on the Celestia icon on

the desktop

❷ First Screen

Once Celestia has started you will find yourself located above earth:

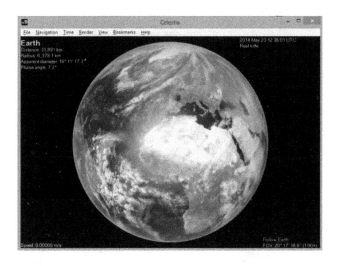

3 Finding out Latitude and Longitude of London

To go to a specific location over earth you need its' latitude and longitude. I would suggest using google to find this out.

① Type Google into the URL/ Address bar of your web browser

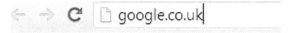

② Type Latitude of London into the search field and press enter

③ Google should provide the information you need:

Make a note of it (it is 51.5072 N, W)

4 Go To London

① Double click on Go To Object in the Navigation Menu

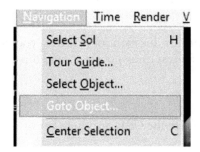

② Enter the Latitude and Longitude of London in the Goto Object

In the dialogue Lat is short for Latitude, and Long for Longitude.

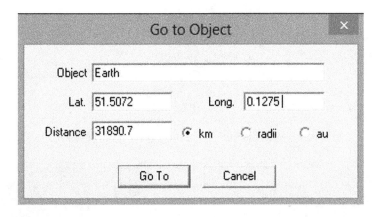

③Enter a sensible distance

For this example I am using 5000 km. Other objects, such as the Sun, might require you to be further away from them to get sensible amounts of detail.

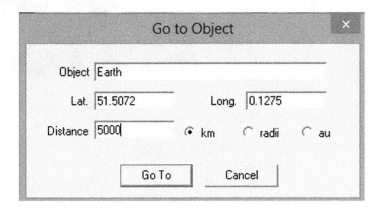

④Press Go To

The Go To Button starts you moving towards your desired location

⑤Press Cancel - This closes the dialogue box

Cancel

You will now see the Britain displayed in the viewable area of Celestia:

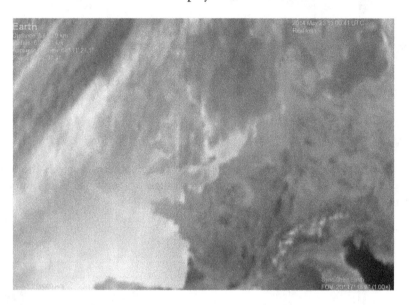

❺Look at the night sky from Above London

Once you've had a good look at Britain you might decide you want to have a good look at the night sky. It's easy to do.

①Click on Select Sol in the navigation menu

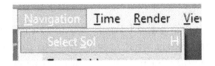

Once you've done this you'll notice that at the top left hand quadrant of the viewing area the selection information changes to read that you've selected Sol / The Sun:

② Click on Center Selection in the Navigation Menu

You will then see the night sky over London as if you were looking directly at the screen.

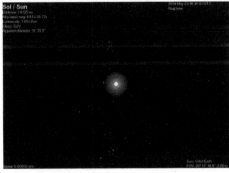

Notice that by holding the left mouse button down and moving to the left or right you can change what appears in your field of view.

However, when you do this the Selection information remains the same.

Your field of view is often independent of your selection. If you want to look directly at your selection use the Center Selection option on the navigation menu.

❻ Go To The Moon

There are several ways to move to a named object which I will describe latter in the book. In this tutorial I will use the Solar System Browser.

① Click on the Solar System Browser in the Navigation Menu

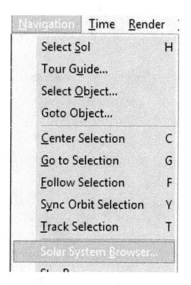

② Expand ⊞ Earth   in the list of solar system objects by clicking on ⊞

③ Select the Moon

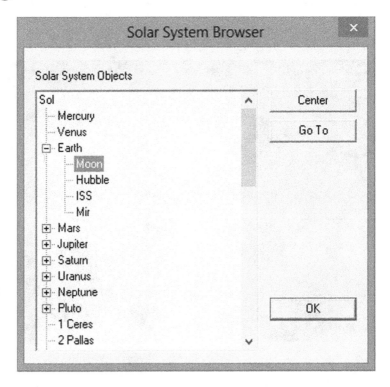

④ Click

You are now looking at the moon from earth.

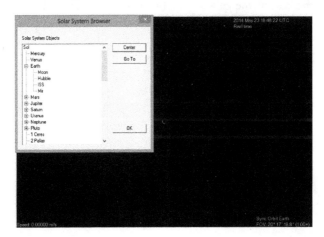

⑤Click ⎡ Go To ⎤ then ⎡ OK ⎤

You have gone to the moon

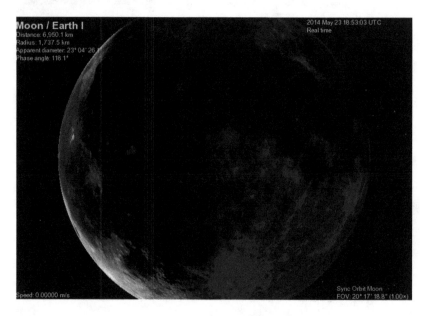

NEXT CHAPTER

Once you've gone to the moon you might be interested in exploring some of the rest of the galaxy. Maybe even seeing what the earth looks like from other planets in the solar system, or the Sun!

4 THE STARS ARE OUR LIMIT

❶ Explore the Moon

① Click on Go To Object in the Navigation Menu

② Adjust Latitude and Longitude

In this example we are going to view Lambert which is at 25.8°N 21.0°W.

Different features are more obvious at different distances. I've selected 4000km for this feature but you can adjust to fit your own screen and inclinations

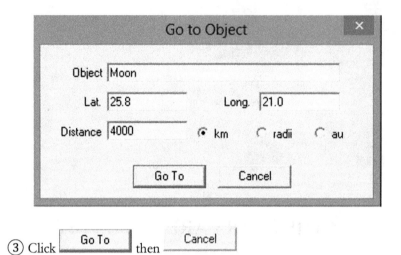

③ Click [Go To] then [Cancel]

④ Press C. This is a keyboard shortcut that centers your selection in

the viewable area. It is equivalent to going Navigation -> Center Selection.

⑤ Lambert will be centered in the viewable area:

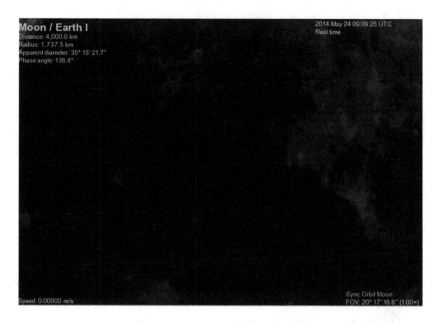

②Looking back at the Earth

① Click on Navigation -> Solar System Browser

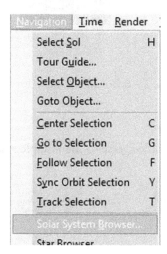

③ Expand by clicking on

④ Select the Hubble

⑤ Select 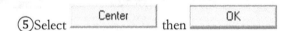 then

You will now be looking at the Hubble space telescope from the moon. Because it's very small, you won't see much except a very small Earth!

⑥ Press G. This is a keyboard shortcut for the Navigation -> Go To

Selection menu item.

Congratulations! You've gone to the Hubble space telescope.

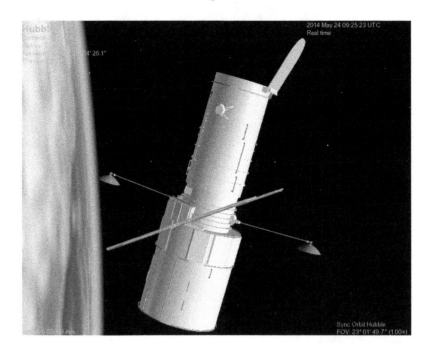

3 Looking at a Star

1 Select the Star Browser from the Navigation Menu

② Select Sol from the list of names

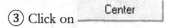

Name	Distance (ly)	App. mag	Abs. mag	Type	^
Sol	1.601e-005	-26.71	4.83	G2V	
Proxima	4.242	11.05	15.48	M5V	

③ Click on ___ Center ___

④Click on ___ OK ___

You're looking at the Sun from the Hubble space telescope. You can look at other stars, too.

⑤ Select Proxima from the list of names

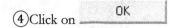

Name	Distance (ly)	App. mag	Abs. mag	Type	^
Sol	1.601e-005	-26.71	4.83	G2V	
Proxima	4.242	11.05	15.48	M5V	
Rigil Kentaurus A	4.365	0.01	4.38	G2V	
Rigil Kentaurus B	4.365	1.34	5.71	K0V	

⑥ Click on ___ Center ___

⑦ Click on ___ OK ___

So… Where's Proxima? If you're lucky you can see it in the viewable area.

Sometimes, however, you won't be able to. It'll be hidden by earth.

Celestia obeys the laws of physics so if something's in the way you won't see what you want to see!

4 Go to Proxima

① Select Proxima on the list of names

Name	Distance (ly)	App. mag	Abs. mag	Type	
Sol	1.601e-005	-26.71	4.83	G2V	
Proxima	4.242	11.05	15.48	M5V	
Rigil Kentaurus A	4.365	0.01	4.38	G2V	
Rigil Kentaurus B	4.365	1.34	5.71	K0V	

Star Browser — Center — Go To

② Press [Go To] then [OK]

You are now located at Proxima

5 Listing the Nearest Stars with Planets

①Click on the Star Browser in the Navigation Menu

②Click on ⊙ With planets in the Star Search Criteria

```
┌ Star Search Criteria ──────────────────────────────────┐
│                                              ⊙ Nearest   │
│  Maximum Stars Displayed in List      100                │
│                                              ⊙ Brightest │
│        ───────┬──────────────────────                    │
│                                              ⊙ With planets│
└─────────────────────────────────────────────────────────┘
```

③Notice that the list of Star names has changed

Name	Distance (ly)	App. mag	Abs. mag	Type	⌃
Sol	4.242	0.40	4.83	G2V	
Gliese 674	11.31	8.78	11.08	M2V	
EPS Eri	12.39	4.09	6.20	K2V	
Gliese 832	14.08	8.36	10.19	M1V	
IL Aqr	15.96	10.28	11.84	M3V	
Gliese 581	18.61	10.34	11.56	M3V	
Gliese 667 C	19.13	9.93	11.09	M1V	
Fomalhaut	24.64	1.12	1.73	A3V	
61 Vir	25.15	4.51	5.08	G5V	
Gliese 433	25.9	9.57	10.07	M2V	
HIP 57443	26.61	4.62	5.06	G3	

6 Listing the Brightest Stars at your current location

Note that nearby stars may not be as bright as distant stars depending on the intensity of the star.

(1) Click on ⚬ Brightest in the Star Selection Criteria

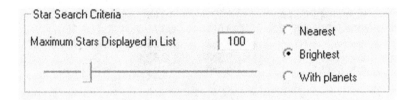

(2) Notice that the Star List has changed again

❼ Refreshing the Star List

(1) In the [Star Browser...] select Sirius B from the list of

stars

(2) Click on [Go To]

Notice that the star list has not changed

Name	Distance (ly)	App. mag	Abs. mag	Type
Proxima	1.07e-006	-21.94	15.48	M5V
Rigil Kentaurus A	0.2051	-6.63	4.38	G2V
Rigil Kentaurus B	0.2048	-5.30	5.71	K0V
Sol	4.242	0.40	4.83	G2V
Barnard's Star	6.569	9.77	13.25	M3V
V1216 Sgr	8.218	10.09	13.08	M3V
CN Leo	8.231	13.65	16.64	M5V
SCR J1845-6357 A	9.021	16.68	19.47	M8V
SCR J1845-6357 B	9.021	30.71	33.50	T6V
Sirius A	9.336	-1.25	1.47	A1V
Sirius B	9.336	8.62	11.34	DA2
EPS Ind A	9.649	4.24	6.89	K4V

③If you want Celestia to update the star list so it shows the nearest,

brightest, or nearest stars with planets to your current location click on
Refresh

The Star list will change to reflect your current position

Name	Distance (ly)	App. mag	Abs. mag	Type
Sirius A	0.0004825	-22.68	1.47	A1V
Sirius B	5.034e-008	-32.72	11.34	DA2
Procyon A	5.252	-1.32	2.65	F5IV
Procyon B	5.251	9.01	12.98	DA
V577 Mon	5.467	9.24	13.12	M4V
Gliese 234 B	5.467	12.32	16.20	M7V
UGPS 0722-05	5.479	34.06	37.94	T9
Luyten's Star	5.664	8.17	11.98	M3V
Kapteyn's Star	7.467	7.69	10.89	M2VI
EPS Eri	7.836	3.10	6.20	K2V
Sol	8.583	1.93	4.83	G2V
GJ 1061	8.977	12.46	15.26	M5V

7Viewing planets around another star

①Press H to Select Sol then G to Go To Selection. This will return us

to our solar system.

② Open the Star System Browser by clicking Navigation -> Star

System Browser

③Click on ⊙ With planets in the Star Search Criteria

Star Search Criteria

Maximum Stars Displayed in List   100   ○ Nearest

○ Brightest

⊙ With planets

④ Select Il Aqr from the Star List

Name	Distance (ly)	App. mag	Abs. mag	Type	^
Sol	7.357e-006	-28.40	4.83	G2V	
EPS Eri	10.48	3.73	6.20	K2V	
Gliese 674	14.82	9.37	11.08	M2V	
IL Aqr	15.21	10.18	11.84	M3V	
Gliese 832	16.14	8.66	10.19	M1V	
Cl EO1	20 67	10 57	11 EC	M0V	

⑤Press   Go To   and   OK

You will see the star IL Aqr on the screen. There are several bright dots
around it – the planets!

⑧Taking a close look at planets in other Star Systems

①Run the Solar System Browser by clicking on it in the Navigation

menu

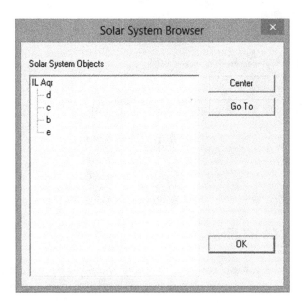

Notice that there is a list of planets that apply to the current star –

not to Sol or our Solar System!

② Select c

③ Click on 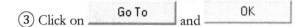 and

You are now viewing the Planet C of IL Aqr.

NEXT CHAPTER

So far in the tutorial we have explored the Solar System, and travelled to stars and even planets throughout the Galaxy. But Celestia doesn't just have to render the universe as it exists today.

In the next section I'm going to explain how to control Time Travel in Celestia so that you can see the Universe as it existed yesterday... or a thousand years ago... or how it will exist in a thousand years' time!

5 TIME CONTROL IN CELESTIA

❶Looking at the sky from Earth in 1066.

①If you are not in the solar system press H and then G to go to the

sun

②Click on Select Object in the navigation menu

③ Type Earth into the Object Name field

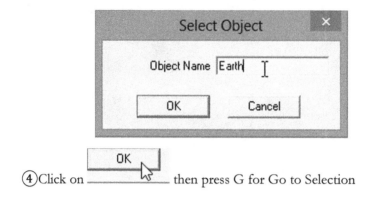

④Click on _____ then press G for Go to Selection

You will be located above earth. Look at the right hand corner of the screen.

2014 May 24 15:37:09 UTC
Real time

It tells you the date that Celestia is currently rendering at the top, and how fast time is flowing below the current time.

⑤Goto Set Time in the Time menu

⑥A Set Simulation Time dialogue will appear. Click on the year field.

⑦Type 1066 and press enter

⑧Look at the time information again. Notice anything different?

Yeah, you've guessed it. You're displaying a simulation of the universe in 1066.

⑨Press H and C to select and center the sun.

You see the night sky as it would have appeared from earth in 1066.

⑩Repeat steps ⑤ and ⑥ but with the current year.

Notice that the sun suddenly disappears from the center of the screen.

This is because the sun was in a different position in the sky in 1066 than the present day. By setting the time you are looking from the same place and direction you were in the past but you'll notice the stars, sun, and planets are all in different locations.

❷Showing the Orbits of planets

It is easiest to see the effect of speeding up and slowing down time by watching the orbit of planets. This section is a bit ahead of the schedule of the tutorial but I hope that you will have patience!

① Select the sun (press H) and Center it (Press C)

②In the Render menu click on view options

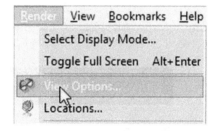

③In the View options dialogue check the Orbits checkmark

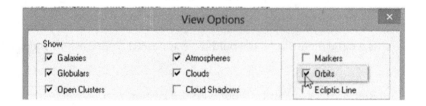

④Press Enter

You will see a large number of blue lines. These are Orbit lines. They are used to show orbits that the planetary objects are making (in this case around the sun).

⑤Take notice of the distance on the left hand top corner of the screen.

Press the END key (normally found on the right hand side of your keyboard over the numbers) a couple of times. Notice that you are moving further away from the sun. Keep on pressing it until you are around 1200 au from the sun. If you go too far, press the HOME key to get closer to the sun.

❸ Make Celestia's simulated time go faster

①Click on 10x faster in the Time menu

Notice that  appears near the bottom left hand of the screen and the time information on the top right hand says

78357 Mar 18 08:17:22 UTC
10× faster

② Watch the seconds changing on the top right hand corner. Time is

travelling ten times faster in the simulation!

③You can also speed up time by using the shortcut L. Press L four

times. You'll see small balls moving along the orbit line – the planets! If you press L again they will move faster still.

④ Make Celestia's simulated Time go slower

①Click on 10X Slower in the Time Menu

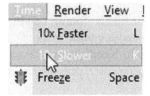

②Celestia should display how fast time is flowing in the top left hand

side of the viewable area.

③You can also slow down time by using the shortcut K. This makes

celestia's time go 10x slower.

5 Freeze Time

Pausing Celestia is easy.

① Click on Freeze Time in the Time menu

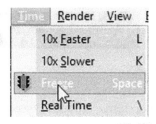

② Celestia will display that time has been frozen in the top right hand

side of the viewable area

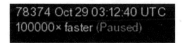

③Click on Freeze time in the Time Menu again. Celestia will resume

rendering with the same time as before you paused.

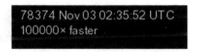

④Pause time again by pressing the space bar. This is a keyboard

shortcut for Freezing time. Then press K, which makes normally makes
Celestia go 10x slower. Time is Frozen, but Celestia has reduced the how

fast it would render time if we had not already Frozen it.

> 78375 Mar 11 13:32:39 UTC
> 10000× faster (Paused)

⑤Resume time by pressing the space bar. Celestia will resume

rendering at the new speed.

> 78375 Mar 11 19:44:58 UTC
> 10000× faster

❻ Set time to Real Time

Real time is where Celestia renders 1 second for every second that passes in the normal universe.

①Select Real Time in the Time menu

You will notice that the time information changes to:

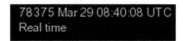

②Press L to make time go 10x faster. Then press the key \ . This is the

shortcut key for freezing time.

7 Going Backwards in Time

Celestia isn't limited to rendering forwards in time. It can do things that the real universe can't do. It can show what the universe would look like if it was going backwards in time.

①Press L five times to make time go faster.

Watch the direction the planets are moving in.

②Select Reverse Time from the Time Menu

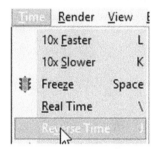

Notice that the Time Information on the right hand side of the viewable area shows a minus sign.

And that the planets are going in the wrong direction. This is because Celestia is rendering the display like a video in rewind.

③Click on Reverse Time in the Time menu again.

Notice that the minus sign on the Time Information is gone.

The planets are going in the right direction again. You're going forward in time.

④Press key J. Time has reversed again. This is because J is a shortcut

key for Reverse Time.

❽Set Time to Current Time

Sometimes when you've been messing with time you might find that you're hundreds or thousands of years away from the present. There's a handy method of setting time to the current time that will save you a lot of hassle.

①Click on Set Time in the Time Menu

②Click on ⌷⌷⌷⌷⌷⌷ Set To Current Time ⌷⌷⌷⌷⌷⌷ in the Set Time

Dialogue.

③Click on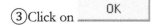

Note that in the Time Information on the top right hand side of the viewable area you can now see the current date and time displayed:

You may be going forward or backwards in time, at real time, or faster or slower than real time. None of those things will change as a result of setting to current time. So, it is often a sensible precaution to freeze time before setting to current time. You can Freeze time by using the space bar then make sure you've given Celestia the right Time settings before pressing the space bar again.

❾Setting to Local Time

Local Time is the time you'd see in a clock at your latitude; Universal Time is the current time at the zero degree meridian (sometimes known as Greenwich Mean Time in the United Kingdom). As a rule it is better to use Universal Time but Celestia does provide the ability to display and use local time.

①Click on Goto Object in the Navigation menu

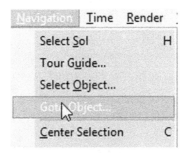

②Enter the following information into the Go To Object Dialogue

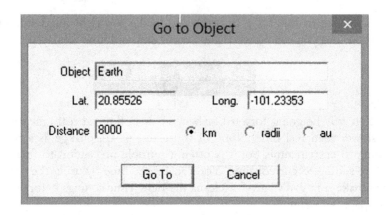

③Click  and

④Click on Show Local Time on the Time Menu

⑤Notice that Show Local Time will have a tick by it

And that the Time Information will read differently

2014 May 24 19:40:48 DST
Real time

The time should match what your computer says on the system clock for your particular time zone.

NEXT CHAPTER

In this chapter we've shown you how to use Celestia to simulate the universe at faster or slower speeds than real time, how to show time flowing backwards, how to set time to whatever you like.

The next chapter will discuss how to control how Celestia Renders the universe, allowing you to change the resolution of the screen, how Celestia renders textures and the light in shadows and how many stars Celestia displays.

6 CONTROL HOW CELESTIA RENDERS OBJECTS

This chapter is a short one focusing on how to control the amount of detail Celestia renders. It shows how to reduce the resolution of the screen, increase or decrease the number of stars, increase the amount of detail Celestia renders about objects in shadow, and control Antialiasing.

Often the default settings will be adequate but if you're having problems with how Celestia is rendering the universe the information in this section could be very useful to you.

❶ Controlling the resolution of the screen

① Click on Select Display Mode in the Render menu

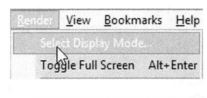

② Click on the ▼ in

62

You can see a list of resolutions. You start with Windowed Mode. This provides good results for most people.

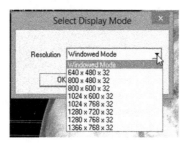

③Find out your screen resolution.

In windows 8, right click on the desktop and select screen resolution

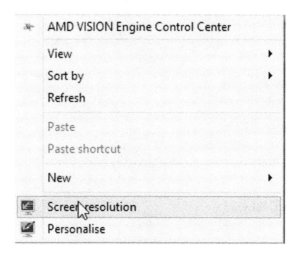

④ A screen Resolution dialogue will appear. Look for the resolution

setting and take note of it

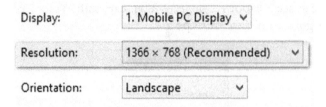

⑤In Celestia, choose the resolution closest to your screen resolution:

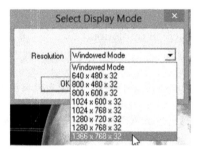

Note, you can set the resolution to anything lower than the screen resolution, but there is no point going for a higher resolution.

⑥Click 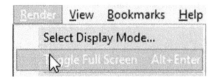. You will go into full screen mode at the

resolution you selected.

⑦Move the mouse to the top of the screen. The Menu bar appears.

You click on Render -> Toggle Full Screen to return to Windowed mode

⑧Alternatively, hold down Alt and press Enter to toggle between full

screen and Windowed Mode.

❷Make Fewer Stars Visible

Celestia allows you to control the number of stars visible by a feature called Auto-magnifier. What you see when you look in Celestia's viewable area is similar to looking through a telescope.

①If you are not already in the solar system, go to it (Press H then G),

go to the earth (Navigation->Select Object Earth, then OK, then press G), then Centre the sun (Press H then C).

②Click on Fewer Stars Visible

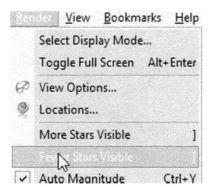

③If you notice less stars, congratulations, but sometimes you need to

repeat the process. Press the key [which is the shortcut for Fewer stars visible until you notice less stars.

④Hold down [until things no longer change. There is a lower

boundary for Auto-magnifier that Celestia sets because it generally doesn't make sense to go beyond it.

⑤You can remove this boundary by toggling Auto Magnitude OFF by

clicking on Auto Magnitude in the render menu.

⑥Press [until there are almost no stars left in the sky. You'll notice that

there is still a limit on how few stars Celestia will show.

⑦You can restore the Auto Magnitude feature by holding down ctrl

and pressing Y. You can toggle it on by pressing ctrl and Y when it's off.

❸Make more stars visible

①Click on [More Stars Visible] in the [Render] menu.

②Alternatively, press the key].

③Again, Auto-Magnitude will limit the degree of magnification. You can toggle it on or off by holding down ctrl and pressing Y. Celestia still has a maximum amount of magnification it will allow even if you disable Auto-magnitude.

❹ Controlling the appearance of stars

So far we've used Celestia's default style for rendering stars. There are two other. options. Rendering stars as points will display the sky in a similar way to many star maps. Displaying stars as Scaled Disks allows you to see how bright stars are compared to each other in the night sky.

①Click on Render->Star Style->Points

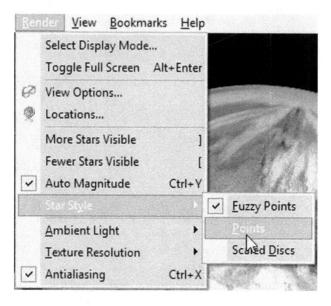

Notice that the appearance of stars in the night sky has changed.

②Click on Star->Style->Scaled Discs in the Render menu

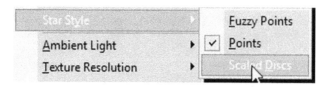

Notice that the night sky has again changed.

③Click on Star Style->Fuzzy Points in the Render Menu

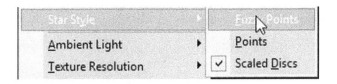

Your display should change back to the original setting.

Experiment with this feature a bit – there are things that are easier to see depending on what star style you use.

❹ Controlling Ambient Light

Ambient Light is an option in Celestia because although Space is a vacuum and there is therefore little reflected light in the universe, dark shadows reduce the amount of detail you can see quite substantially.

①Go to the Moon (Select object Moon, OK, press G)

②Click on Navigation->Go To Object to bring up the Go To object

dialogue

Enter the Following Data:

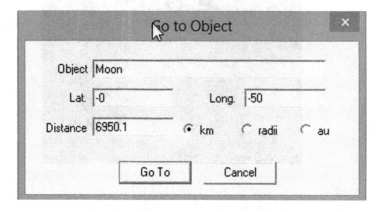

③Press 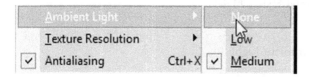 then

④Click on Ambient Light -> None in the Render Menu

⑤Note how little detail there is in the shadows of the moon.

⑥Click on Ambient Light->Low in the Render Menu

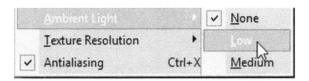

⑦Notice there is more detail in the Shadows of the moon

⑧Click on Ambient Light->Medium in the Render Menu

⑧Notice the level of detail in the Shadow portion of the moon.

I often use the Medium setting for Ambient light in Celestia since I like the additional amount of information that this displays.

5 Controling Texture resolution

Celestia displays objects like planets by mapping information it stores about them onto textures. The higher the resolution on those textures the smoother they appear. If you use lower resolutions they can be very blocky, if you use higher resolutions they can appear too smooth.

As a rule of thumb I suggest leaving the default settings, but it is possible to alter them.

①Click on Texture resolution->Low in the Render Menu

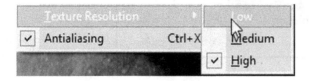

②Notice that the surface of the moon has become very blocky

③Click on Texture Resolution->Medium in the Render menu

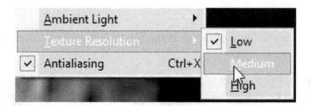

④Notice that the surface of the moon has become smother

⑤Click on Texture Resolution->High in the Render Menu

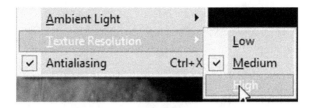

⑥The surface of the moon has become very smooth

I often find that medium is the best setting but it really does depend exactly what you want to see and also on your monitor and personal taste! Experiment and see.

6 Antialiasing

Antialiasing is a graphics technique that can help when Celestia renders objects that are moving. It smooth's out the movement but at the expense of some fuzziness. I recommend that you leave Antialiasing at its default setting. But if you are having trouble rendering movements properly it does sometimes help to turn it off.

①Click on Antialiasing in the Render Menu to turn it off

②Alternatively, Hold Ctrl and press X.

③Repeat step ① or ② to toggle Antialiasing on or off.

NEXT CHAPTER

In this Chapter we've discussed settings that control HOW Celestia renders the universe, in the next chapter we will discuss settings that allows Celestia to display mapping information on planets and other terrestrial bodies.

7 INFORMATION ABOUT TERRESTRIAL BODIES

Celestia often displays information that you can't "see" in the real universe. You've already seen one example of that – when we turned on the show orbits feature. You can also make Celestia display labels that show information about features, grid lines, constellation and star names and many other features.

There are two main types of information that Celestia can display:

Information about planets and other terrestrial bodies such as moons and asteroids.

Information about stars and other interstellar bodies.

This chapter will focus on the first type of information. It will describe how to show labels about cities, mountains, valleys, land masses and many other forms of information. It will also show how to use the limit size feature so that information doesn't get crowded out.

❶Showing Labels

①Go To Earth

Select Object "Earth", OK, press G

②Go To London

Click on Select Object in the navigation menu
Enter London

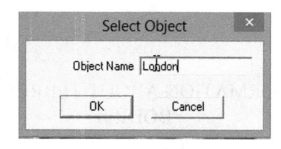

Press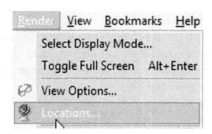

Press G

③Click on Locations in the Render Menu

④ You are in the Locations dialogue.

There are many features that are selected already, including Cities, observatories, landing sites etc. But none of these items are showing up as labelled in Celestia.

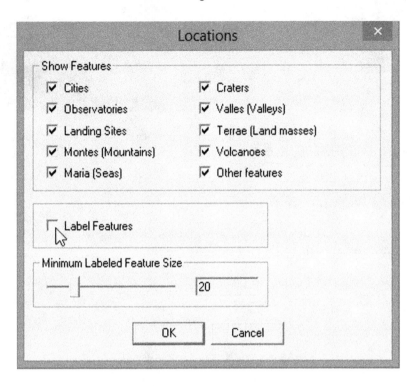

⑤Turning on Labels

Check the Label Features option

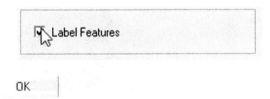

Press   OK

The dialogue should close.

⑥Notice that the Earth has changed:

The Earth is now covered in a large number of labels. Celestia includes capital city names by default.

2 Toggle City Labels on and off

Celestia can label all capital cities on the globe.

①Open the Locations dialogue box by clicking

Locations... in the Render menu.

②In Show Features there is an item called ☑ Cities . To turn off city labels, click on the ☑ until it shows ☐ Cities .

To toggle it back on click ☐ Cities on the square again.

3 Toggle Observatories on and off

There are no observatories in the default installation of Celestia. It's a default category that you can add information to latter on.

① Open the Locations dialogue box by clicking

in the Render menu.

② In Show Features there is an item called Observatories . To turn off

Observatory labelling, click on the ✔ until it shows ☐ Observatories .

③ To turn on Observatory labelling, click on the ☐ until it shows

Observatories

4 Toggle Landing Sites Labels

①Open the Locations dialogue box by clicking

 in the Render menu.

②In Show Features there is an item called 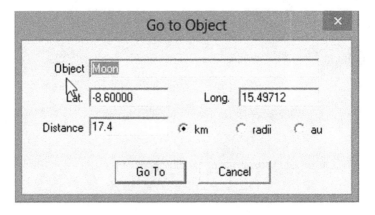Landing Sites . To turn off

Landing Site Labels, click on the ☑ until it shows ⌐ Landing Sites .

③It's easiest to see landing sites on the moon. Go to the following

latitude

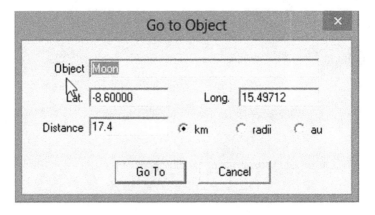

You are at the Kiva landing site, but since labelling landing sites is turned off you see:

④To turn on Landing Site Labels, click on the ⌐ until it shows

☑ Landing Sites

⑤Landing sites tend to be quite small, so you will have to reduce the

minimum labelled feature size to 20 in order to see them

When the Labeled Feature size is low enough, you see the Kiva landing
site labelled:

● 5   Toggle   Montes

(Mountains) Labels

①Open   the   Locations   dialogue   box   by   clicking

▨ Locations... | in the Render menu.

②In Show Features there is an item called ☑ Montes (Mountains) . To turn

off Montes (Mountain) Labels, click on the ☑ until it shows

⌐⅄ Montes (Mountains) .

③ Goto the moon

Go to Object ✕

Object [Moon]

Lat. [-8.60000]   Long. [15.49712]

Distance [4446.8]   ⊙ km   ○ radii   ○ au

[Go To]   [Cancel]

④You will not see any Mountains labelled

⑤To turn on Montes (Mountains) Labels, click on the ⌐ until it

shows ⅄ Montes (Mountains)

⑥ Make sure you reduce the Minimum Labeled Feature Size enough

that you can see the labels

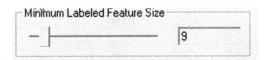

6 Toggle Marias (Seas) Labels

①Open the Locations dialogue box by clicking

 in the Render menu.

②In Show Features there is an item called ⋈ Maria (Seas). To turn off

Maria(Sea) Labels, click on the ✔ until it shows ⌐ Maria (Seas) .

③Goto the moon

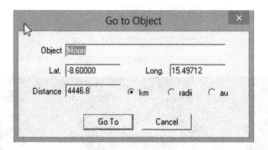

There shouldn't be any Seas labelled

④To turn on Marias (Seas) Labels, click on the ⌐ until it shows

 Maria (Seas)

7 Toggle Craters Labels

①Open the Locations dialogue box by clicking

 in the Render menu.

②In Show Features there is an item called 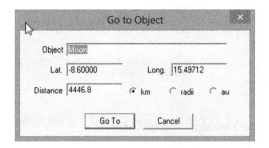Craters . To turn off

Crater Labels, click on the ✔ until it shows ☐ Craters .

③Goto the moon

There shouldn't be any craters labeled

③To turn on Craters Labels, click on the ☐ until it shows ✔ Craters

Make sure that the Minimum Labelled Feature Size is reasonable

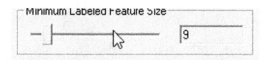

8 Toggle Valleys Labels

①Open the Locations dialogue box by clicking

 in the Render menu.

②In Show Features there is an item called ☑Valles (Valleys) . To turn off

valley Labels, click on the ☑ until it shows ☐ Valles (Valleys) .

③Go to the Moon

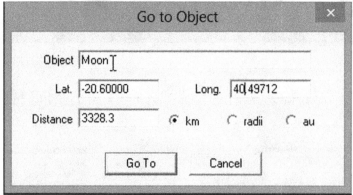

You shouldn't see any valleys labelled

④To turn on Valley Labels, click on the ⌐ until it shows

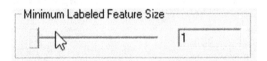

Valleys are very small features. Make sure the Minimum Labbeled Feature Size is set very low

You should see the valleys labelled

![valleys labelled image]

9 Toggle Terrae (Land Masses) Labels

①Open the Locations dialogue box by clicking

![Locations button] in the Render menu.

②In Show Features there is an item called ☑ Terrae (Land masses) . To

turn off Terrae (Land Masses) labels, click on the ☑ until it shows ⌐ Terrae (Land masses) .

③Go to Earth (Select Object in Navigation menu, press OK, Press G)

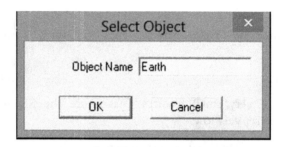

④Select North America

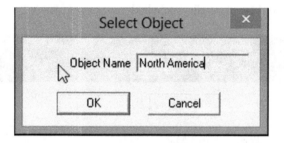

Press OK, then G (to Go to Selection)

④You won't see the Land Masses labelled

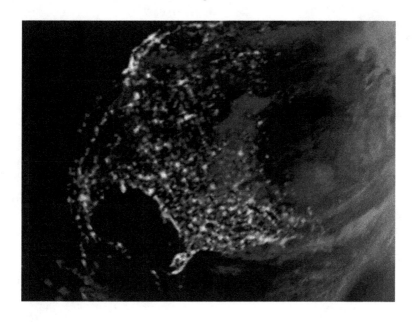

⑤To turn on Terrae (Land Masses) Labels, click on the ⌐ until it

shows ☑ Terrae (Land masses)

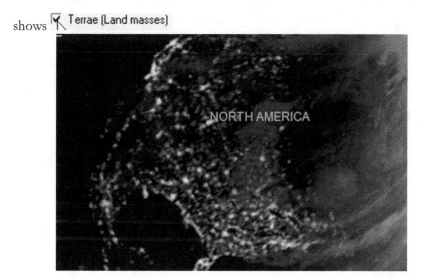

❿Toggle Volcanos Labels

There aren't any Volcanos stored by Celestia by default, it gives you this option in case you want to expand the data Celestia stores later.

①Open the Locations dialogue box by clicking

 in the Render menu.

②In Show Features there is an item called ☒ Volcanoes . To turn off

Volcano Labels, click on the ☑ until it shows ☐ Volcanoes .

③To turn on Volcanos labels, click on the ☐ until it shows

☒ Volcanoes

⓫Toggle Other Labels

THIS IS ANOTHER DEFAULT CATEGORY FOR CELESTIA WITHOUT DATA.

①Open the Locations dialogue box by clicking

 in the Render menu.

②In Show Features there is an item called ⟨image⟩ Other features . To turn off

other planetary labels, click on the ✔ until it shows ☐ Other features .

③To turn on other labels, click on the ☐ until it shows

⟨image⟩ Other features

⑫Minimum Label feature Size

Celestia allows you to control the minimum size of the features that you label. It does this through the Locations menu. Without the ability to control this size you'd often get occasions where there were so many labels that they would be illegible

①Click on  in the Render menu

②See the Minimum Labeled Feature Size option.

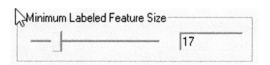

③Slide 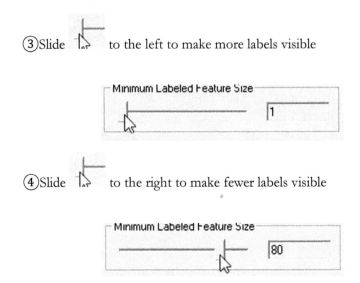 to the left to make more labels visible

④Slide to the right to make fewer labels visible

The screen will update as you change this feature allowing you reasonably fine control over the number of labels that you show.

NEXT CHAPTER

In this chapter we've shown you how to map the surface of planets and other terrestrial bodies. You've learned how to control the minimum feature size so that more or less labels are visible, and you've also learned that you can often use Select Object to go to a labelled feature.

In the next chapter you will learn how to use Celestia to display information about the rest of the universe.

8 INFORMATION ABOUT THE REST OF THE UNIVERSE

This chapter will show information about how to use Celestia to display cloud cover, grid lines, orbit lines and many other things that might be of interest to you when you are using Celestia to display the universe.

Some of the features are also useful because the default installation of Celestia gives you information such as weather patterns that may get in the way of displaying information that you might want.

❶ Toggle galaxies on or off

① Click on  in the menu

② In Show there is an option called ☑ Galaxies to turn Galaxies off,

click on the ☑ until it shows ☐ Galaxies and then press   OK

It is easiest to see the effect from outside the Milky way. Click on Go To in the Navigation menu and enter the following:

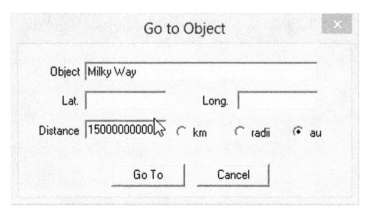

Followed by [Go To] and [Cancel]

When Galaxies are off you will see:

③To turn on Galaxies, click on the ☐ until it shows ☑ Galaxies and

then press [OK]

Go to the above coordinates. When Galaxies are on you will see:

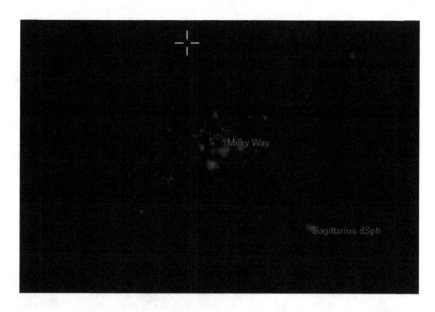

❷ Toggle Globulars on or off

① Click on View Options... in the Render menu

② In Show there is an option called ☑ Globulars to turn Globulars

off, click on the ☑ until it shows ☐ Globulars and then press OK
To see the effects go to Select Object in the Navigation menu

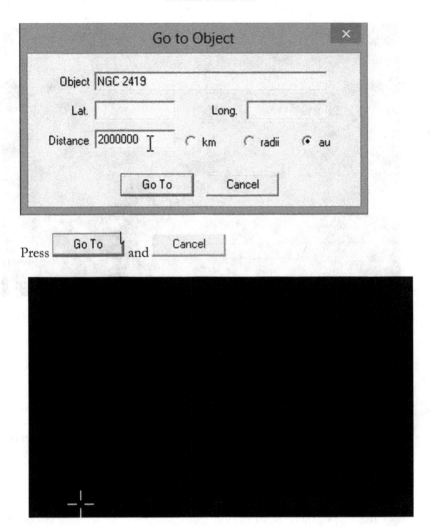

Press and

③To turn on Globulars, click on the until it shows ✔ Globulars and

then press OK

At the above coordinates you will see

❸ Toggle Open Clusters on or off

OPEN CLUSTERS ARE AN OPTION THAT CELESTIA PROVIDES TO ALLOW YOU TO EXPAND THEIR BASIC DATABASE.

① Click on  in the menu

② In Show there is an option called ☑ Open Clusters to turn X off,

click on the ☑ until it shows ☐ Open Clusters and then press OK

③ To turn on Open Clusters, click on the ☐ until it shows

☑ Open Clusters and then press OK

4 Toggle Nebulae on or off

NEBULAE ARE AN OPTION THAT CELESTIA PROVIDES TO ALLOW
YOU TO EXPAND THEIR BASIC DATABASE.

(1) Click on  in the menu

(2) In Show there is an option called ☑ Nebulae to turn Nebulae off,

click on the ☑ until it shows ☐ Nebulae and then press OK

(3) To turn on Nebulae, click on the ☐ until it shows ☑ Nebulae and

then press OK

5 Toggle Stars on or off

(1) Click on in the menu

(2) In Show there is an option called ☑ Stars to turn Stars off, click on

the ☑ until it shows ☐ Stars and then press ⬚ OK

To see the effect of toggling this click on Go To Object in the Navigation menu

Enter the following:

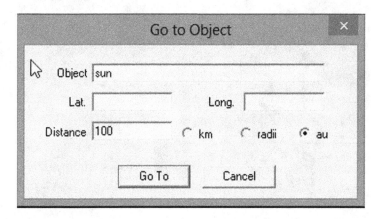

Click on ⬚ Go To then ⬚ Cancel

With the stars turned off you will see

③To turn on Stars, click on the ☐ until it shows ☑ Stars and then

press

At the above coordinates with stars turned on you will see

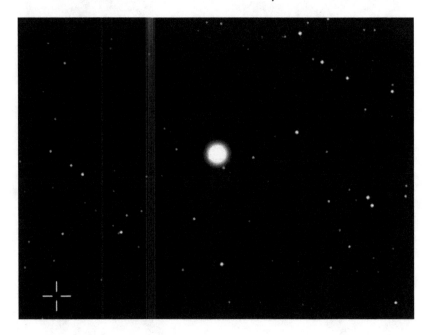

Note that the sun is considered a star in astronomy and so when you turn off stars in Celestia you also turn off the sun!

❻ Toggle Planets on or off

① Click on  in the **Server** menu

② In **Show** there is an option called ✔ **Planets** to turn Planets off, click on the ✔ until it shows ☐ **Planets** and then press [OK]

To see the effects of this, click on Go To Object in the Navigation menu

Enter the following data:

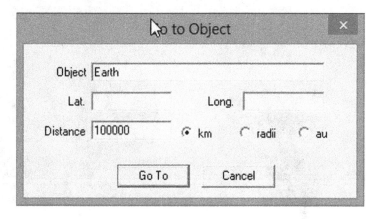

Press  and then

When planets are off you will see

At the above coordinates you will see

④Now, see the effect of turning off planets on moons.

In Show there is an option called ☑ Planets to turn Planets off, click on the ☑ until it shows ☐ Planets and then press [OK]

Click on Select Object in the navigation menu
Enter the following data:

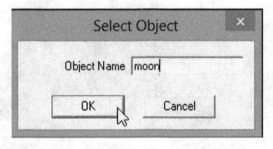

And press [OK]

Press the key G to Go To selected object
This is what you will see:

If you switch on planets (described above) you will see the moon.

This is really an error in Celestia; there should be an option to switch of planets and a separate option to turn off planetoids.

7 Toggle Atmospheres on or off

① Click on  in the ⟨Render⟩ menu

② In **Show** there is an option called ☑ Atmospheres to turn

Atmospheres off, click on the ☑ until it shows ☐ Atmospheres and then press OK

To see the effect of this click on select object in the navigation menu
Enter the following data

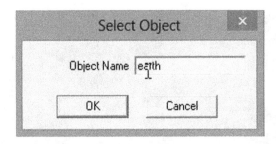

Press 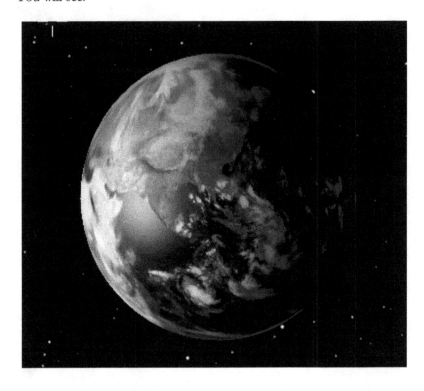 OK

Press G to Go To the object, and if necessary the home key until you have a good view of the earth (make sure that the show planet option is

checked from step ❻ otherwise you won't see the earth!)

You will see:

③To turn on Atmospheres, click on the 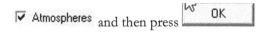 until it shows

☑ Atmospheres and then press [OK]

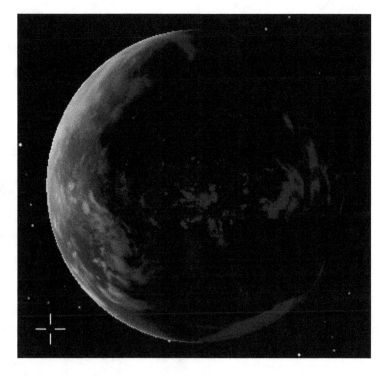

It might be hard to make out the difference in the book copy but you should notice that the more of the surface of the earth is brighter with atmosphere on. This is because the atmosphere is scattering light.

❽Toggle Clouds on or off

① Click on  in the Render menu

② In Show⌐ there is an option called ☑ Clouds to turn Clouds off,

click on the ☑ until it shows ⌐ Clouds and then press ⌐ OK ⌐

To see the effect of this Click on Go To Object in the navigation menu and enter the following data:

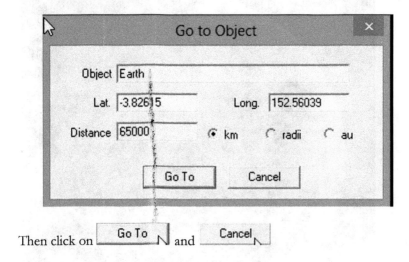

Then click on Go To ∧ and Cancel ∧

You will see the Earth without cloud cover:

③To turn on Clouds, click on the ☐ until it shows ☑ **Clouds** and then

press ☐ **OK**

At the above coordinates you will see the earth with cloud cover:

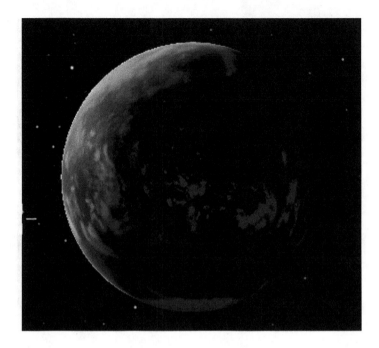

9 Toggle Cloud Shadows on or off

Is turned off by default

① Click on  in the ⟍ menu

② In Show⟍ there is an option called ☐ Cloud Shadows to turn Cloud

Shadows on, click on the ☐ until it shows ☑ Cloud Shadows and then press ⟍ OK

It's very difficult to show the effect in print because the resolution isn't good enough. Instead, I recommend you try it yourself at a reasonable distance from the Earth!

You will see that with cloud cover on, the surface of the earth will be much darker.

③To turn on Cloud Shadows, click on the 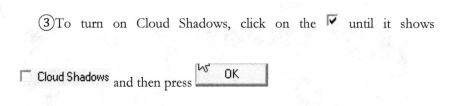 until it shows

☐ Cloud Shadows and then press [OK]

❿Toggle Ring Shadows on or off

① Click on  in the [Render] menu

② In Show there is an option called ☑ Ring Shadows to turn Ring

Shadows off, click on the ☑ until it shows ☐ Ring Shadows and then press [OK]

So see the effect click on go to object in the navigation menu and enter the following data

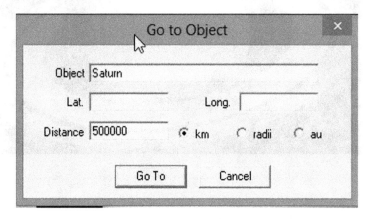

Click on [Go To] and then [Cancel]

With Ring Shadows off you will see:

③To turn on Ring Shadows, click on the ⌐ until it shows

☑ Ring Shadows and then press [OK]

To see the effect of turning Ring Shadows on go to the above coordinates. You will see

⑪ Toggle Eclipse Shadows on or off

① Click on  in the ⟍ menu

② In Show⟍ there is an option called ☑ Eclipse Shadows to turn Eclipse

Shadows off, click on the ☑ until it shows ☐ Eclipse Shadows and then press ᵂˢ OK

To see the effect of this option you will have to go to a time and place that has an eclipse.

Select Eclipse Finder in the Navigation menu.

Make sure that you enter the following information:

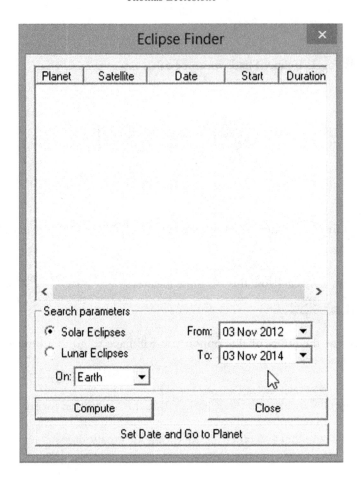

Click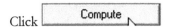

The list of eclipses will be populated. Select the first eclipse

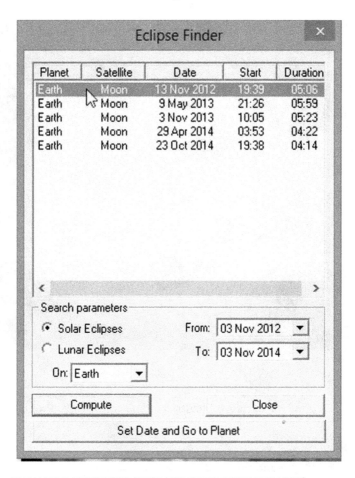

Press

Set Date and Go to Planet

Press the End key to get a decent view of the earth. You will see

③To turn on Eclipse Shadows, click on the ⌐ until it shows

☑ Eclipse Shadows and then press [OK]

Note that the shadow will move across the earth as the eclipse progresses.

⓬ Toggle Night Side Lights on or off

① Click on  in the ▔▔ menu

② In Show there is an option called ☑ Night Side Lights to turn Night

Side Lights off, click on the ☑ until it shows ☐ Night Side Lights and then press ☐ OK

To see the effect of this option select Go To Object and enter the

following data

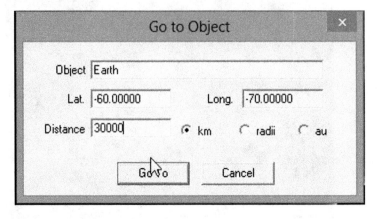

Click on  and then Cancel

Select Set Time in the Time menu

Enter the following data

Press

You will see the earth at night time without any lights rendered

③To turn on Night Side Lights, click on the ⌐ until it shows

☑ Night Side Lights and then press [OK]

At the above coordinates and time you will see the earth rendered with lights

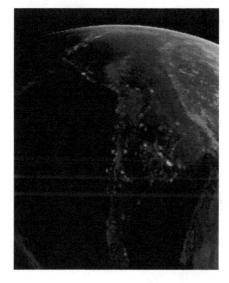

⓭ Toggle Comet Tails on or off

① Click on  in the ⌐ Render ⌐ menu

② In ˙Show˙⌐ there is an option called ☑ Comet Tails to turn Comet

Tails off, click on the ☑ until it shows ⌐ Comet Tails and then press ⌐ OK

Comet tails are shown by Celestia in proportion to the comets size and are always shown facing away from the sun. Because Celestia doesn't have many comets stored in its database you wouldn't normally see a comet tail but it is possible to expand the Celestia database in which case this option might be more useful.

③ To turn on comet tails, click on the ⌐ until it shows ☑ Comet Tails

and then press ⌐ OK

⓮ Toggle All Orbits and Orbit Labels on and off

Orbits are artificial lines that Celestia uses to show the path that planets, asteroids and other objects are following through space. Celestia allows you to control Orbits at both a general and a specific level; i.e. you can turn all orbits on and off or you can turn individual classes of labels on and off.

①To turn all labels click on view options in the Render menu

②On the right hand side there is the following set of options

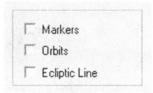

③ Click on the ▯ next to ⌐Orbits until it shows ☑ Orbits then press

To see the effect click on Go To Object in the Navigation menu
Enter the following data

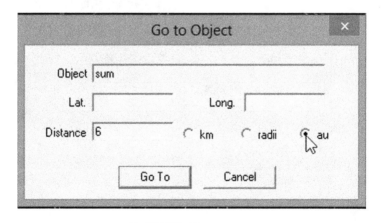

Press Go To and Cancel .
You will see

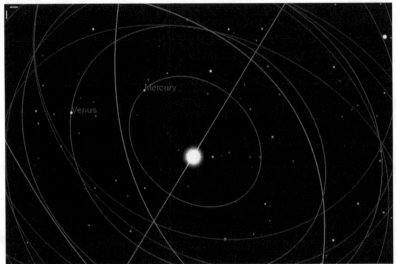

Note that depending on your individual selections of individual classes

of objects to label (see point ⑮) this may vary.

④ To toggle it off click on view options in the render menu, look on

the top right hand corner of the view options dialogue and click on the ☑

until it shows ⌐⟍ Orbits then press OK

You will see:

The decision to choose not to show orbits overrides any of the

individual class options you have selected in point ⑮ and you will simply

not see any orbits.

⑮ Toggle individual classes of Orbits and Orbit Labels on and Off

We've already seen how to turn off Orbits and Orbit Labels generally. If Orbits are on you can also toggle specific Orbit types and Orbit Labels types. This allows you to see, for example, planetary orbits but not the orbits of space stations.

Before these options have any effect, you must toggle all Orbits and

Orbit Labels to on. Instructions on how to do this are in step **⑭**.

① Click on  in the Render menu

②In the Bottom left hand corner are the Orbit and Orbit Label

options:

③The Orbit options are the check box on the far left. On the above

screenshot, for example, the Stars orbit option is on, and the orbit label
option is off. The planets Orbit option is on, and the Planets Orbit Label
option is also on.

To toggle an Orbit on click on ☐ until it shows ☑. To turn an Orbit
off do the opposite.

④ Orbit labes give you a text description of the object the Orbit relates to. You can turn it on by toggling the second check box. For example  means that the Stars Orbits but not Orbit labels are showing. means that you have told Celestia to show Orbit Labels for stars.

⑯ Toggle DSO Labels on and off

DSO stands for Deep Space Object. Celestia can show the international designation for objects like Galaxies and Nebulae.

① Click on   Options...   in the   Render   menu

② On the Right of the Orbits/ labels option are the DSO Labels

options. They look like:

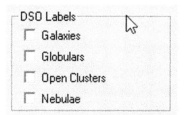

③ To turn on a label for a particular class of objects click on the ⌐ ɪ

until you see ✔ . For example, ✔ Galaxies means that you are showing labels for galaxies .

④ To turn off a label for a particular class of objects click on ☑ until

you see ⌐ ʀ. For example ⌐ **Open Clusters** | means that you are not labelling open clusters.

⑰ Toggle Grids On and Off

Celestia allows you to see astronomical grids. These grids can be especially useful when you are using free flight, or when you want to identify a particular location in the night sky from earth.

① Click on  in the Render menu

② The Grids options are on the right of the show options under the

Marker, Orbits and Ecliptic line options. They look like:

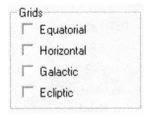

③ While it is possible to show more than one type of Grid at a time I

recommend that you only use one. To turn on a Grid click on the ⌐ until it shows 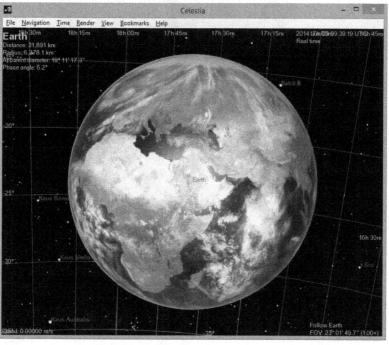. For Example ✓ Equatorial means that the Equatorial Grid is on.

④To turn off a grid click on ✓ until it shows ⌐. For example,

⌐ Equatorial. means that the Equatorial grid is off.

⑱Toggle Constellation options On and Off

Celestia has the ability to show the following information about constallations

A diagram, connecting up the stars within a constellation to make it clearer

The borders of the constellation, showing a rectangle in the sky that includes all the stars in that constellation

Label naming the constellation
The Latin name of the constellation

① Click on 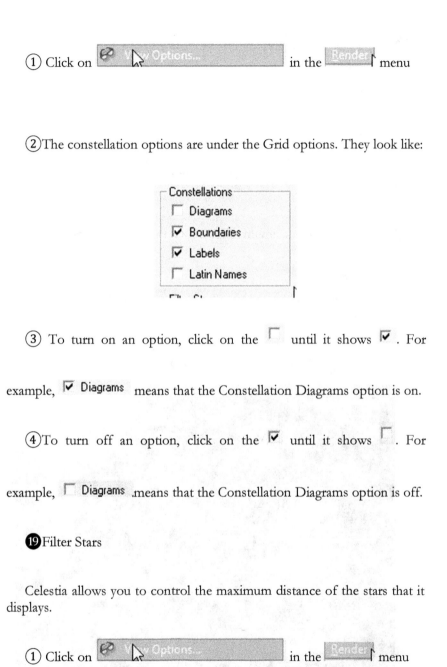 in the Render menu

② The constellation options are under the Grid options. They look like:

Constellations
☐ Diagrams
☑ Boundaries
☑ Labels
☐ Latin Names

③ To turn on an option, click on the ☐ until it shows ☑ . For

example, ☑ Diagrams means that the Constellation Diagrams option is on.

④ To turn off an option, click on the ☑ until it shows ☐ . For

example, ☐ Diagrams .means that the Constellation Diagrams option is off.

⑲ Filter Stars

Celestia allows you to control the maximum distance of the stars that it displays.

① Click on in the Render menu

②The Filter star options is on the bottom right hand corner of the

screen and looks like:

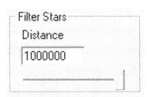

③To reduce the maximum distance of the stars you can move the

slider from the right hand side ——————————— to the left hand side

④The further to the right the scroll bar is, the more stars you see:

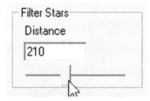

Displays

⑤I generally recommend keeping the maximum number of stars visible

20 Markers and Ecliptic Lines
Markers are a celestia option that makes it easier to see an object

① Click on  in the Render menu

② In the top right hand corner of the screen is the Marker, Orbits and

Ecliptic lines options. It looks like:

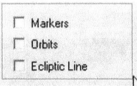

③To turn Markers on, click on the □ until it looks like ☑ Markers

④Select an object, for example press H then C to centre the sun

Notice that your selected object is now marked.

⑤You can toggle markers on or off by pressing ctrl-K. Press Ctrl-K

once. Notice that the Sun is no longer marked.

NEXT CHAPTER

In this chapter I have discussed some of the ways that you can control what Celestia displays on the screen. You can control what labels Celestia displays, what objects it displays, as well as the number of stars and many other features.

In the next chapter I will describe how record screen captures and videos within Celestia as well as some other features.

9 SCREEN CAPTURES', VIDEOS AND OTHER RESOURCES

In this chapter I will show you how to take screen shots and videos in Celestia as well as many other miscellaneous features in Celestia. I will also give you hints of where you can find out more about extending and automating the program.

❶ How to take screen captures

When you are using Celestia you may sometimes want to record screen shots for documentation or other purposes. Celestia provides you with a screen capture function for precisely that purpose.

① In the **File** menu click on **📷 Capture Image...** **F10**

② Select the directory in the normal way, and enter the file name

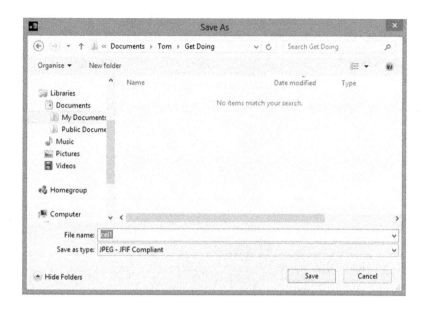

③Make sure that the Save as Type is JPEG – JFIF Compliant

④Press

②How to record a video

①In the File menu click

②Select the directory in the normal way and type in the file name

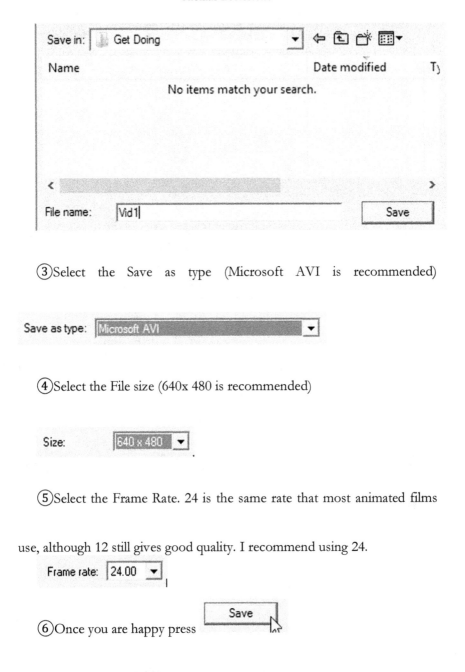

③Select the Save as type (Microsoft AVI is recommended)

④Select the File size (640x 480 is recommended)

⑤Select the Frame Rate. 24 is the same rate that most animated films

use, although 12 still gives good quality. I recommend using 24.

⑥Once you are happy press

⑦The Video compression dialogue is displayed. I recommend keeping

the settings at the default

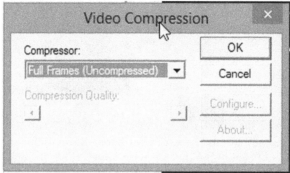

⑧You will note a red square appears in the main viewing area

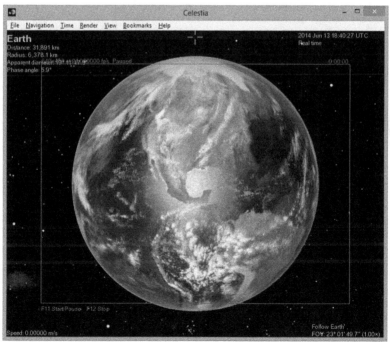

Celestia will record everything within the rectangle

⑨ Navigate to the place you want to start the movie

⑩ To start recording, press F11. Once started the top right hand

corner of the red rectangle will show █ Recording █. To pause it, press F11

again and it will show █ Paused █.

While recording you can use Celestia like normal, but the program will make a video of everything that happens within the red rectangle.

⑪ Press F12. The red rectangle will disappear, and the movie file will

be saved automatically.

❸Running User Guide

The user guide is written in html, so you will need a functioning web browser set up before you can use it.

①In the . Help menu click on 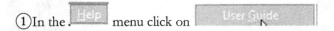 User Guide

②The celestia user guide will appear in a web browser window

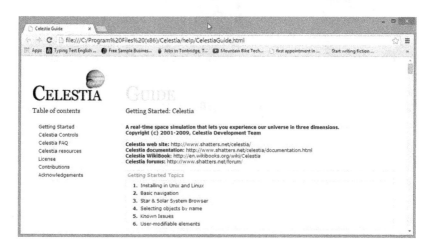

❹Running the Demo

Celestia provides you with a demo that shows you some of the highlights of the program. It's easy to run and actually quite good fun to watch!

①In the  menu click on

②The Demo will start

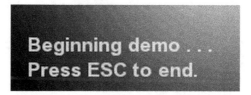

③ To stop the demo press ESC on the top left hand corner of the

keyboard.

5 Information on keyboard, mouse and joystick control key codes

Celestia gives you a list of keyboard shortcuts and hints and tips on how to navigate using the mouse in this handy dialogue.

①In the [Help] menu click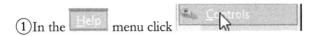

②Scroll down until you reach the option you want.

③Click [OK] to close the dialogue.

6 Information about OpenGL and Celestia licenses

I guess that some people might be interested in the legalities of the program… one for the lawyer geeks!

①Celestia uses the OpenGL library to render graphics. To find out the

license terms for OpenGL click on [OpenGL Info] in [Help] menu

②To find out Celestia's licensing information click on

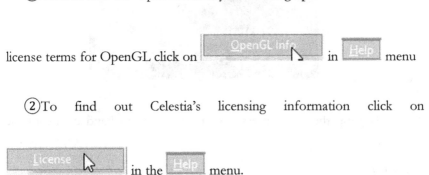 in the [Help] menu.

7 Information on Celestia

To find out current version number and information about the team that designed celestia click on [About Celestia] in the [Help] menu.

8 Running Standard Scripts

Celestia provides a few standard scripts. This is Mark Local Group Galaxies and Show Redshifts of Galaxies.

Please note: when running scripts you often make permanent changes to the appearance of the viewable area within Celestia. I advise you to make sure that you bookmark your current location if you want to find it again because you will need to restart celestia if you want it to return to the normal appearance.

① To Mark Local Group Galaxies goto the [File] menu hover the

mouse over [Scripts ▸] then click on

[Mark Local Group Galaxies]

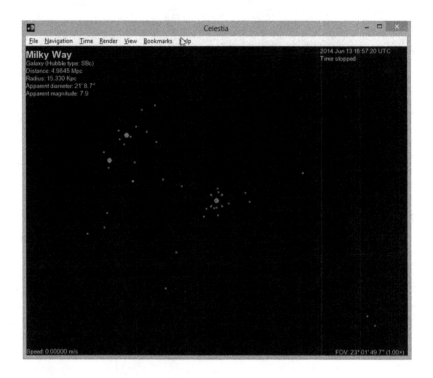

②To Show Redshifts of Galaxies, goto the  menu hover the

mouse over Scripts then click on

Show Redshifts of Galaxies

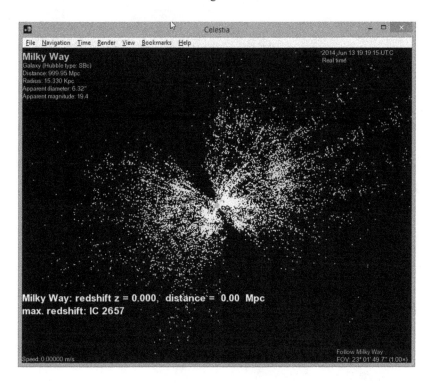

9 Finding out more about Celestia

That's the end of this Beginners Guide To Celestia. But before I go, there are several resources that you will find very useful if you want to continue to learn more about the program, in particular how to extend it and how to write scripts for it.

Celestia Web Site: http://www.shatters.net/celestia/

Celestia User Forums: http://www.shatters.net/forum/

Selden's List of Resources for Celestia: http://www.lepp.cornell.edu/~seb/celestia/

Celestia Wikibook: http://en.wikibooks.org/wiki/Celestia

Celestial Matters Website and Forums: http://www.celestialmatters.org/

http://forum.celestialmatters.org/

Celestia   **Motherlode:** http://www.celestiamotherlode.net/

I hope that this beginners guide has been useful, thanks for taking the time to read it and don't forget to send me any hints about how I can improve it at thomasecclestone@turingsbrain.com

Good luck!

ABOUT THE AUTHOR

Thomas Ecclestone is a software programmer and technical writer from kent in the south east of England. In his spare time he looks after a herd of hebridean sheep, and lives on a smallholding in kent, and writes books.

You can find out more about his current projects at thomasecclestone.co.uk

www.ingramcontent.com/pod-product-compliance
Lightning Source LLC
Chambersburg PA
CBHW071002050326
40689CB00014B/3455